Good Night,
Indiana University

Good Night, Indiana University

Written by **Joey B. Lax Salinas**

Illustrated by **Prabir Sarkar**

Illustrations based on
photography by **Joey B. Lax Salinas**

INDIANA UNIVERSITY PRESS

To my children, Parker and Madelyn

Good night Sample Gates, the door to IU

With grand limestone arches
the students walk through

Good night Rose Well House
on the IU Old Crescent
Among vibrant oak trees
and a sky opalescent

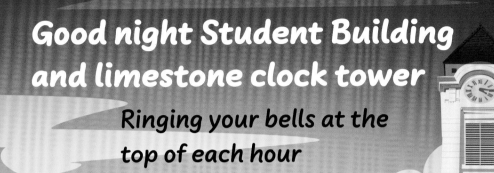

Good night Student Building and limestone clock tower

Ringing your bells at the top of each hour

Good night Dunn's Woods with your high hickory trees

With a kaleidoscope of leaves blowing free in the breeze

Good night Beck Chapel
where students come to pray

And where some
will choose to have
their wedding day

**Good night Campus
River winding past
Woodburn Hall**

Good night wooden bridges
and minnows so small

Good night Showalter
Fountain, spraying
mist in the air

From Venus to the
dolphins and fish
swimming there

Good night IMU and fun things to do

Like bowling and movies with delicious food too

Good night crimson clocks,
keeping students on time

Playing "Indiana, Our Indiana"
on your beautiful chime

Good night Auditorium
and red balcony seats

Listening to rock
concerts with rockin'
band beats

Good night Musical Arts Center,
please dim your light

Good night ballet, opera,
and performances at night

Good night Arboretum
and wide open spaces
Walking past so many other
smiling students' faces

Good night Grand Carillon
and your sixty-five bells

Ringing from the Arboretum
to President Herman B Wells

Good night Wells Library with your books stacked so tall

Filled with so many students studying throughout the hall

Good night Kirkwood Observatory,
looking up at the stars

Viewing distant planets
like Jupiter and Mars

Good night Memorial Stadium, good night Hep's Rock

The game is now over, no time on the clock

Good night Assembly Hall,
where championships are won

Where the history is rich
and the atmosphere fun

Good night Kirkwood Avenue and store window lights

Good night delicious restaurants and late-night bites

Von Lee

Good night Bloomington, from up in the clouds

Above Lotus Fest, Pride Fest, and other big crowds

Good night cream and crimson
under a bright crescent moon

Good night Indiana University,
in my dreams I'll see you soon.

Indiana University Terms

THE ARBORETUM is an open space and arbor park located in the center of campus at the site of the former Tenth Street Stadium. Remnants of the former stadium can still be seen all around the Arboretum.

ASSEMBLY HALL (officially, Simon Skjodt Assembly Hall) is the home of Indiana University's men's and women's basketball teams. Opened in 1971, Assembly Hall has hosted numerous big-ticket events from speeches to rock concerts, in addition to thousands of basketball games.

THE AUDITORIUM is the primary entertainment venue located near the center of campus. Opened in 1941, the Auditorium has hosted countless events including traveling Broadway plays, politicians, comedians, and rock stars such as Bob Dylan and John Mellencamp.

BECK CHAPEL is a non-denominational church located next to Dunn Cemetery. Built in 1956, Beck Chapel often serves as a wedding venue for alumni and staff.

CAMPUS RIVER is a small creek that flows from east to west through the heart of the Indiana University campus.

DUNN'S WOODS is a wooded area in the southwest corner of campus and was part of the original twenty acres purchased in 1883 when IU moved to its present location from Seminary Square.

GRAND CARILLON is a bell tower at the center of the Arboretum. Built in 2020, the Metz Bicentennial Grand Carillon replaced the Metz Carillon that was originally located on Seventeenth Street near IN-45/46.

KIRKWOOD AVENUE is one of the primary business districts in Bloomington and connects the downtown square to the campus. Many popular retail stores and restaurants are located along Kirkwood Avenue, and it is the center for much of Bloomington's nightlife.

KIRKWOOD OBSERVATORY is IU's very own astronomical observatory. Built in 1900, the observatory is still used today in undergraduate classes.

HERMAN B WELLS was Indiana University's eleventh president and first university chancellor. A statue erected in his honor just east of the Sample Gates greets students in a plaza that is named for him.

IMU, short for Indiana Memorial Union, is a building located near the center of campus. It is home to many facilities including dining halls, a movie theater, a bowling alley, a billards room, the IU Bookstore, and the Biddle Hotel.

LOTUS FEST refers to the Lotus World Music and Arts Festival held annually in downtown Bloomington, Indiana.

MEMORIAL STADIUM is home to the men's football team at Indiana University. Opened in 1960, the stadium is also used for other events, such as graduation ceremonies.

MUSICAL ARTS CENTER (MAC) is a performance space for the IU Jacobs School of Music's Opera and Ballet Theater and also home to IU recording and production facilities. The Musical Arts Center seats over fourteen hundred guests and has advanced acoustical designs that make it a grand and desirable place to enjoy a performance.

THE OLD CRESCENT borders Dunn's Woods and is the oldest area of the Indiana University campus. The first buildings on the campus are here, including IU's first two buildings, Owen Hall and Wylie Hall, as well as Kirkwood Hall, Lindley Hall, Maxwell Hall, the Frances Morgan Swain Student Building (often refered to by its original name, the Student Building), Franklin Hall, and the Rose Well House.

RED CLOCKS are located in various locations around the Indiana University campus, primarily in high foot traffic areas. The clocks play music at the top of the hour.

ROSE WELL HOUSE is a stone arched gazebo located in the Old Crescent on the Indiana University campus. Built in 1908 as the first cistern on campus, it holds two original stone portal gates from the Old College Building, one of the original IU buildings on the Seminary Square campus.

THE SAMPLE GATES are among the most recognizable landmarks on the Indiana University campus and have been the image most often used when referencing Indiana University. Built in 1987 where Kirkwood Avenue once entered the campus, the Sample Gates have become one of the most popular locations on campus to take a photo or a selfie.

SHOWALTER FOUNTAIN is located at the center of the Fine Arts Plaza, surrounded by the Fine Arts Building, the Auditorium, and the Lilly Library. Showalter Fountain has been the site of many celebrations and protests over the years including war protests and national championship celebrations. The fountain features a statue of the goddess Venus being born from a clam shell surrounded by dolphins and fish.

THE STUDENT BUILDING, renamed the Frances Morgan Swain Student Building in 2016, is located on IU's Old Crescent just east of the Sample Gates. Standing tall since 1905, the Student Building's clock tower rings its bells at the quarter of every hour.

WELLS LIBRARY is the main campus library located near the center of campus just east of the Arboretum. The exterior of the library's two main sections resemble stacked books. Formerly known as the Main Library, the Wells Library was renamed in 2005 to honor IU's eleventh president, Herman B Wells.

About the Author

Born and raised in northwest Indiana, **JOEY B. LAX SALINAS** is an Indiana University graduate with a bachelor of arts degree in telecommunications. Since graduating from Indiana University in Bloomington, he has worked as a photographer and video producer and has continued to return to the Bloomington campus to photograph campus landmarks and buildings and various changes that occur on campus over the years. In 2018, Joey became an official licensed photographer of Indiana University, taking photos covering all Indiana University campuses.

In addition to Indiana University photos, Joey has also captured photos and created photo galleries for nearly every city and town in the state of Indiana. Today, he continues to add more cities to his photo gallery collection, including photos of the Chicago suburbs, western Michigan, northern Michigan, and beyond. You can see some of his work at www.joeylaxsalinas.com.

This book is a publication of

Indiana University Press
Office of Scholarly Publishing
Herman B Wells Library 350
1320 East 10th Street
Bloomington, Indiana 47405 USA

iupress.org

Manufactured in China
Production Location: Shenzhen, China
Production Date: 4-28-2023
Cohort: Batch 1

First Printing 2023

Library of Congress Cataloging-in-Publication Data

Names: Lax Salinas, Joey B., author, photographer. | Sarkar, Prabir (Illustrator), illustrator.
Title: Good night, Indiana University / written by Joey B. Lax Salinas ; illustrated by
    Prabir Sarkar ; illustrations based on photography by Joey Lax Salinas.
Description: Bloomington, Indiana : Indiana University Press, [2023] |
    Audience: Ages 0-5 years | Audience: Grades K-1
Identifiers: LCCN 2022057911 (print) | LCCN 2022057912 (ebook) | ISBN
    9780253067029 (Hardback : alk. paper) | ISBN 9780253067043 (eBook)
Subjects: LCSH: Indiana University—Juvenile literature. | Bedtime—Juvenile
    literature. | Moonlight in art. | Picture books for children.
Classification: LCC GV885.43.I53 S35 2023 (print) | LCC GV885.43.
    I53 (ebook) | DDC 378.772/255—dc23/eng/20230216
LC record available at https://lccn.loc.gov/2022057911
LC ebook record available at https://lccn.loc.gov/2022057912

For Indiana University Press

Emily Baugh Editorial Assistant

Tony Brewer Artist and Book Designer

Brian Carroll Rights Manager

Dan Crissman Trade and Regional Acquisitions Editor

Samantha Heffner Trade Acquisitions Assistant

Brenna Hosman Production Coordinator

Katie Huggins Production Manager

Darja Malcolm-Clarke Project Manager/Editor

Dan Pyle Online Publishing Manager

Nancy Smith Artist and Book Designer

Stephen Williams Marketing and Publicity Manager